The Much Love Sad
Dawg Trio Matt Sadler

The Much Love Sad Dawg Trio

Copyright © Matt Sadler 2010, 2017, 2018

Cover design: Mary Sadler

All rights reserved. Including the right of reproduction in whole or in part in any form.

This book is published by **DYNAMO VERLAG**

Capitol Hill, D.C., Echo Park, Los Angeles, and Seattle

Printed in the U.S.A.

9 8 7 6 5 4 3 2 1

Dynamoverlag.com

DYNAMO VERLAG

ECLECTICISM | GENIUS | ORIGINALITY

The Much Love Sad Dawg Trio Matt Sadler

Acknowledgments

The author wishes to acknowledge the following publications, in which the work presented here has previously appeared:

Poetry Center of Chicago's website, www.poetrycenter.org, which first published "Letter to Myself"

Salt River, which first published "Letter to Layne from Tucson" "Faint Music," "The Blue Glow Of," "New Year's Pig," and "Waxwing"

MetroTimes, which first published "Bubble Wrap and Packing Foam"

Versal, which first published "Letter to Mary from the Future, Part 1," "Letter to Mary from the Future, Part 2," "Sunburst School," "Because in the Movie They Got It All Wrong," and "Mars Rover Spirit, to Mars Rover Opportunity"

Poetry East, which first published "The Year My Father Grew Potatoes from Potatoes." "Hawk in the Backyard," and "How to Pick Up a Watermelon Seed"

Passages North, which first published "Salt"

Red Ink, which first published "Dreaming at Kyi-Yo"

Some of the work in this book previously appeared in the limited release, handmade chapbook *Tiny Tsunami*, put out by

Flying Guillotine Press

The author wishes to thank the following for their help, guidance, support and love in the making of this book: Tony Mancus, Sommer Browning, Frank Montesonti, Melissa Koosman, Mike Sadler, Andrew and Katie Bode-Lang, and Megan Garr.

This book is for Mary and Anna and Gretchen.

Contents

Introduction by Frank Montesonti 13

I.

Bubble Wrap and Packing Foam 17
Waxwing 19
Letter to Mary from the Future, Part 1 20
Letter to Mary from the Future, Part 2 22
Ode to Architecture 24
Letter to Myself 26
Imperative..28
Letters to Trees 30
Letter to Layne from Tucson...33

II.

How to Pick Up a Watermelon Seed 37
The Year My Father Grew Potatoes from Potatoes 39
Salt...41
Sunburst School...43
Dreaming at Kyi-Yo..44
Hawk in the Back Yard 46
The Self 48
The Blue Glow of 50

III.

Mars Rover Spirit, to Mars Rover Opportunity 53
The Much Love Sad Dawg Trio 56
Vision 66
Turning Thirty 67
In Accordance with the Prophecy 69
Concert Posters 71
Faint Music 73
Because in the Movie The Got it All Wrong 74
Muting 75
Benediction 76
When I come up with a new idea 77
New Year's Pig 80

About the Author 85

Introduction

Frank Montesonti

I am so very glad to see *The Much Love Sad Dawg Trio* reissued. Because of the untimely passing of the book's publisher, this first collection of poems by such an uber-talented poet received far less recognition than it deserved.

How do I describe a Matt Sadler poem? When I read a Matt Sadler poem I feel a slow brightening in my head. It's a warmth that leads to a sudden awakening, like the speaker in "Letters to Trees," where Sadler writes "I'm listening to Brahms again and the cello sounds almost happy this time/and the light through the window forms a perfect triangle/ on the brown carpet and the whole room is this new apple/ we're living on."

The poems in *The Much Love Sad Dawg Trio* are the difficult combination of being reverent and humble. It is not the "look at me being humble" type of humility of Christianity, but the quality of mind of someone almost inexhaustibly willing to inhabit a world before passing judgment.

It's like Matt Sadler's mission is to start his own religion not beholden to the "do's and don'ts, for-the-lord-/hath-saids, and other forced wisdoms." (Imperative, 14). His poems wake and wake again, but unlike Buddhism, they don't need to quash the self or desire. In the poem "Dreaming at Kyi-Yo" where the speaker's feels compelled to dance until self and dance are one.

The poems continually wonder how at human kinds endless ingenuity of self-creation. In one poem, Sadler tells a parable of a bag of potatoes that left alone in a cupboard began multiplying, reminiscent of our uniquely human ability "to make something out of nothing" (26).

These lovely poems from *The Much Love Sad Dawg Trio*, not only brighten my head, but also spur me to action. After I read this book I find myself turning toward the window to notice the cerulean blue sky behind the pine forest. I feel my body suddenly restless to leave the house and walk around the neighborhood for no good reason except to notice the world again.

In "Letter to Layne from Tucson," he writes, "I'd like to be held like that again,/ if only in your mind, with care and utility" (19). And ultimately, that is what I love so much about this collection, its care and utility, the way it holds the world.

I

Bubble Wrap and Packing Foam

And what did you do with yourself today? The sun
closes its empty eyelids, the unemployment line breaks for a meal,

the janitor jangles his giant ring of keys. Doesn't it seem he
    could unlock
anything? Why doesn't he go into the vault and come out wealthy?

Can he at least tell you what *you're* trying to unlock? You watch
with disinterested attention as the skeleton of a culture is laid open

one careful fistful at a time. The hearth a scattering of broken ceramic,
the fired clay colored ground mustard seed and pomegranate.

And what do you learn about your life? Do you walk across the
    cold rail bridge
toward home, kicking stones through the vertiginous slats,

lit by the subtle grace of inspiration? Did you pay your respects?
Your insurance bills? Say yes to yourself even once?

At the whale museum, I pass through a giant rib they've made
    into a door,
into the soft plush of the gallery, unscathed

but digested in some important way.
Is it wonder or reverence that opens my heart and my wallet

and I'll buy a sweatshirt and some postcards, please.
And if we are related to that first scaled dog that drug itself
    out of the sea,

that would explain our awkwardness and our grace, our eczema,
    our gills.
Someone found one off a coast somewhere, now chest pinned open,

studied and explained. But I want everything explained,
 all at once if possible.
Dissect the coffee shop and the wormy dirt, label each node of
 the brain,

walk along the terminal moraines of our existence and expertise.
Feeling unbeatable, I pop into the video store and buy the special
 edition extended play

double platinum directors cut. You go back to your office and dream of
 surgical heroism,
of inventing a giant plug for the giant hole everyone's talking about.

Then you get back to your work. What else can you do but participate?
And hope, when you come home and the mail comes, there's a package

with your name on it? And don't you wrap yourself up in a package
 every day
only to deliver yourself to your own doorstep at 6, or if you're lucky,

someone else's doorstep, of if you're luckier,
your own with someone else inside who loves you? And don't you tear
 yourself open

together each night, dig through your guts, both expecting, above
 all else,
to find something good in there?

Waxwing

What I need to do is walk out in the snow with my arms folded over
my chest
and look at the bent limbs with consternation.

I'll wait for a thousand waxwings
to sift down through the stillness and air.

I'll wait there three more years until they finally destroy
the Juniper on my back stoop, rise like a snapped sheet

with one old hawk chasing them, or one big crow.
I know at least one of them will slam into my kitchen window,

drunk on the rotten, fermented berries, and slide down pathetic,
cartoon-like; wake up confused,

fly off, and leave me forever. And once is enough. And today
my heart is this ravaged, broken tree, and today I am one great bird

made of a thousand smaller than I, and I can't tell if I'm chasing
or following the others to the next ruin.

Letter to Mary from the Future, Part 1

I've been searching for the beginning and the end of Self in books,
but what are books?

And what is plaster-of-paris? And have you ever thrown an onion
against a red brick wall? And what sound does it make?

If you follow the horizon sideways the sky is always frowning at you.

You say turn it upside down, and we both grow taller
in our attempt to get closer to gods. I show you my teeth

and you pull out the molar of a whale. You wrap up every
piece of coal in the skin of a diamond.

What if the Rockies are the narcissus of the Great Salt Lake?
What if the entire continent was made this way, grown

in the ocean's dim reflection as if in a Petri dish?

What if the night collapses like the edge of some endangered ice shelf,
the ocean a giant, tinkling martini?

Take each idea to its absolute. I've been trying to become an idea.

And you say ideas are like mountain trails, that anyone can attain
the most significant peaks, but no one is allowed to stay there.

And I've been looking for meaningful gestures inside the fixed eye
of the dictionary. Until everything changes

in the next edition, suburbs of language sprout up around us
like a blooming yellow meadow

and the heads turn to seeds and spread everywhere.
Do we run away from explanation?

Do we live inside a new description of each moment?
Are words the end of experience?

You say they only begin the experience, and we blast of this treeline
in a skyrocket juniper for somewhere new to start naming.

Letter to Mary from the Future, Part 2

And I've found all the corkscrews that you turn into wine.

And I've tasted the food I make for poison. And I've lived three lives
inside my worry

and you brush it all away like skin peeling from a sunburn.
And I know that life is the process

of living and dying. And I've been thinking about death, and
within that category, that inevitability, about ours.

What happens when the outside world closes its yawning jaw,
blinks its open eye,

Pompeiis us into our final archaeology?
And when they unearth you in some unimaginable future

you will be the perfect disguise for our mistakes on this planet,
and I next to you curled into knots,

rawhide for skin, mouth open in a scalding testimonial O
as if, in death, I bore witness to their worst fears

about what's involved, what happens to them, what's waiting,
and they look back to you to understand

why I clung so desperately to that life
and this death, and they dream all their dreams there and then,

and they turn to their co-workers and smile about their bright clean world,
and they unfurl their notebooks

like a great blue flag
and mark me down a footnote, new, lucky to have been there.

Ode to Architecture

If I had one more wish I would ask Mies Van Der Rohe
to slip down from his boxy heaven and design me a new self to
 inhabit,

not because I long for sleek modern lines

nor for my liquids to issue forth from the tastefully disproportionate
 new holes
and spouts he'd install, but to feel the words *Mies Van Der Rohe*

slide their easy way between my tongue and the ridges above it,
the kissed *M* at the beginning and the long breathy finish.

I'd take any new self he'd give me, and maybe I'd donate my old self

to charity, do the right thing for once, but more than likely
I'd keep both selves to myself, my extra hanging idly,

a stiff new suit in my schizophrenic closet, waiting for me to shed
my other self and fill it with purpose and form.

One self might say that everything you can possibly imagine must
 already exist

and the other, enraged, may overturn the checkers board
and proclaim that something unknown must exist, possibly creation
 itself.

One might start a church while the other pouts out a couple tunes
on his acoustic guitar. And what a headache

trying to keep them separate, trying to keep them
from pummeling each other into the same oblivion, that
 sticky steamy mess

from which they each emerged into being

as if response itself were some kind of evolution,
as if evolution could disguise itself as wish,

as if such a wish were already happening.

Letter to Myself

To see a person's legs detach and run off in opposite directions
would be funny, right?

I thought so, too. Is the surreal, then,
just another version of this comedy?

What if my brother calls me *puddle* as a joke? (He does).
Should I rip all the mirrors off his Subaru?

Does he even have a Subaru?
This condition, this anti-reality, is becoming the air

around me, is filling the domed hat our planet wears.

And there are fewer and fewer geeky, bespectacled logic birds
clotting the skies each year.

How to explain their decline? Cranial warming? A hole
in the skull cap? Matt, the world is too serious for all this.

But what else can I do? I've heard

that emperors used to pay their underlings handsomely
just to remind them they were mortal, not god. Here

all the mortals have shotguns and fuzzy orange hunting hats,
and my birds drop like the stems of a firework

after a bright round explosion. Logic escapes me.
But the semblance of logic remains, the structure,

the bare holy studs of it. *A* still goes perfectly
with *B*. *Then* ubiquitously follows *If*.

It's no use. I can walk through walls, but transparency
is too vast a realm.

If the quadratic formula sprouts wings,
then it will fly off this rock and leave us alone.

If you see three tomatoes unripening on my kitchen windowsill,
then come into my house, fill it with sadness,

empty your windsock so my kite can rise.
All useless. No sense to it. I've broken

the key off inside the lock.
With any luck

I can find someone to praise me like a king
for minimum wage.

Imperative

What does the self need but
a body to move it here to

here, a heart to heat it up
another heart for love.

And if I've searched my gospel
for clues, I've found only

do's and don'ts, for-the-lord-
hath-saids, and other forced wisdoms there.

And I'm sketched the shapes of leaves,
long and sad and curving,

and I've convinced myself that sanding wood
uncovers, rather than creates

the shine. What does the self need
but a vessel, forcing it into a

shape, a set of rules and definitions
to govern its mysteries,

some mysteries to try to explain.
Like, does the world ache

this sweetly, so full and fleshy
as if in danger of spoiling. Yes.

And we are obsessed with what moves us
here to here.

We give each to each
and light to light, and if

the doctor says
22 years of breathing in

has coated your lungs
with cockroach skin?

At 4 AM, the silver strata,
this is when

I can't help but think
there's something more

buried under these words under each rock
shriveled by past and future and present—

A plastic pot warped by the sun
streaming through the kitchen window every day—

Every sentence a small assassination
of wordless pure thought,

and we, by which I mean we,
ought....

Letters to Trees

I'm listening to Brahms again and the cello sounds almost happy this time
and the light through the window forms a perfect triangle

on the brown carpet and the whole room is this new apple we're all living on.

Today the wife of a good friend had to tell him he wasn't a bad person
and he wouldn't believe her until she stormed from the room,

finally agreeing. He knew he was. Because of something inside him.

Because, for him, that cello only echoed his torture.

Early this week someone, somewhere on a coast caught a lobster 22 lbs—and older, they estimated, than any living human—

and when they moved it too a zoo for us to appreciate, it died there.

Because a place can be what keeps you.

And today I learned the inside of a bubble rising in boiling water
is hotter than the surface of the sun. Something about pressure or physics

and it makes me think those bubbles must have some special purpose,
like delivering the souls of the dying water molecules to their afterlife in the air,

their rebirth in the great atomic cycle, their god's conveyance
    for hot tea.
Because boiling water is one kind of transcendence.

And today people everywhere are planning conservation parks
    in space
and performing surgery on the cataracts of a great horned owl

and eating spicy cabbage and salted plums at the movies and
    drying
and shredding the seaweed.

And someone, somewhere, is building a machine only because
    it is beautiful

and someone else, somewhere else, uses the machine
and doesn't think about its beauty, and the sky ravages
    the world

with just one cold bright color. And because that description
    resembles an eye
looking down.

And because of the early melt and the icicles over the garage like
    an anxious jaw,
and the horizon over the rows of identical rooftops across the street,
    another jaw.

I woke up this morning and heard
the salt crystals crunching under the mailman's boots.

I've seen him before, he's a big man, he could swallow me
if he wanted. And I wonder if he's in love with the world today

or if he's still waiting for his own pillar of light
and his own scalding coffee and his own probably not Brahms to
    beckon him

upward, to let the world enter him like a bright infection
and ravish his large, ready self.

I wonder if his world is bigger than mine
and the thought depresses me, someone else's bigger world, and
   the bones

of an old leaf scrape by against the pavement.

And it sounds like faith walking away.

And did you know the brain has a stem?
And is the brain, then, the fruit of something else toiling far below?

Because writing this is unlike writing any other kind of letter.
What words can save me? Why does transcendence

only seem to go in one direction? Because I begin digging

and always uncover an abyss.
Because I am writing this letter on my own skin.

Because, as I rise, I still feel I have to hack off a small piece of myself
   each day
and kick it, lucky, back into the void.

Letter to Layne from Tucson

First of all, I don't care about the money.
I never have. Today the heat

reminds me of coffee surrounded by sex,
which reminds me of you in some way.

I think in the movie of my life there are
too many panoramic views of birds

flying up and away from the camera.
One of the hardest things I've had to realize

I realized just now, writing this. My distance
has hurt people. I hope you are not one of them.

The predominant tree here grows long, spiral pods
that can be ground into a sweet flour that nobody

ever grinds it into. One common cactus
has large pads that can be eaten as a vegetable.

I hear they are good with eggs. My point is,
there are interesting things everywhere

that no longer fill me. A friend of mine
takes care of a Vietnam vet

who went over the handlebars
of his motorcycle. She lifts him

from his bed and puts him in his chair.
She lifts him from his chair

and puts him back in his bed.
She talks to him, tries to get him

to remember simple, small things.
I guess I'm saying that

I'd like to be held like that again,
if only in your mind, with care and utility.

II

How to Pick Up a Watermelon Seed

First bring me a summer day so hot
the dogs can only lie and pant
naked bellies flat on the cool tile floor,

and bring me the dogs, two loyal shepherds
to guard the melon patch,

a sham vine grown
from a single seed sold to me for a dollar
by a street person promising

seedless melons. I didn't ask the obvious—
how'd he get the seed

to grow a seedless melon?—but then my head
was so full of hope under the
scrutinizing sun and clouds.

Let the melon vine overrun the yard
as the dead do the living, and let us stand

in circles around the flowering garbage can
in the park, spitting our multitude of seeds,
those disembodied teeth, into the center

of that flower.
And let that be a kind of pollination!

I know one stray seed will fall,
because it must, slimily to the concrete
from my lip and, perfect as we

must be, let the girl there
try to pick it up, the seed slipping

from her fingers a hundred times
before she gets it.
And let that girl be my wife, and I,

sham of a man, peeking down her shirt as she struggles
with the seed, let me say

with all the truth I can muster,
thank you and thank you and thank you.

The Year My Father Grew Potatoes from Potatoes

The way my father tells it
it was miracle plain as day
potatoes from nothing, a

virgin birth. And over the bang
and clatter of plates,
the usual restaurant symphony,

and over a pile of fried potatoes,
he always tells it. When he tries
to include the waitress this time

she scratches her head with the tip
of a pencil, leaves
partway through. It is a long

story. The short version, he left
a bag of potatoes in a pantry so long
they rotted, sprouted, and filled

the entire dark and empty space with their
spindly albino shoots.
In the center of which, according

to my father, grew one perfectly round,
golf ball sized Yukon Gold.
I call him a fool. I tell him

that his miracle potato
was nothing more than cannibal,
feasting on it's own,

I tell him that whenever I imagine
an airplane he is always the pilot
and god help us all.

The waitress
comes back, avoids eye contact,
gives us our plates.

Eggs on dry wheat toast,
a little ketchup, a dash
of pepper, the smell of burning hash.

What he really means is to teach me.
And he's clever about it,
I'll give him that.

He has this miraculous ability
to make something out of nothing.
Just like the story. I get it. Okay.

Salt

The man in the picture has a face
like a closed door, white
as a new magazine.

I make a list
of words, changing only one letter
from the word before, and soon

I feel the day slipping like that,
letter by letter. A girl I know
loved salt so much

she got on her knees
and licked the flat dirt ground
beside a highway south of Idaho.

I think the man worked hard,
leaving a trail of worn
wooden handles behind him

on the path his life took.
I write the list of words
in small print across his forehead.

Some animals will seek out anything
a human has touched
and eat it.

The path behind him
might look like that, tangled,
half gnawed.

The girl I know actually told me
that she'd like to see her own
forbidden places. So for her sake

I hope her life goes wrong
in the city. She can stand
with some trees after that,

in some other state, looking back
in the direction she came from.
I can see those trees.

I can see the blue dress
her mother gave her, tight
against her ribs.

Sunburst School

Her first night out in Shelby she lied about her age
and got into bed with a twenty-year-old cowboy named Buck.

She didn't believe his name by the snarl on his lip when he
said it, but she liked the radio station playing rock

and the feeling that the world, this world and then beyond,
all the way to Great Falls, all the way to Spokane,

was finally at her fingertips. She woke up in his apartment
next to the Econolodge tangled in these misted dreams

as if in a sheet, unwrapped herself and made her way to her car
smiling and yawning. When she looked

at the digital clock on the dash
she knew the light that would break over the barren hills

on her way home. To drive back into Sunburst like this
is to hope for crumbling bricks, for rust to gather on the joints

of the oil rigs, for the Post Office to close again, taking away
the last part-time job, for the barley to wither, the moving vans

to rumble in, the government, finally, to sign the check. Here
the feel of a car underneath is almost dangerous,

and the sudden flare of trees around the school, their deranged
branches, like a huge signpost pointing everywhere.

Dreaming at Kyi-Yo

First the blue door and the whistling hinges and my palm pressed flat
against the dented metal,

and two hands holding each other in front of the drinking fountain.
It opens on Earl Oldperson, a crooked smile

like a gourd growing inside a breaking vase. And I am standing next to him.
And I am always the guest of honor.

If I close my eyes now a distant cousin with a gum red beard
will play *Amazing Grace* on the bagpipes,

the bladder contracting in slow accordion folds.

And a man in a top hat will drive the hearse, a Cadillac, slowly through
my town. He'll see the pedestrians

take off their hats and their stares through the dark tinted glass
of the side windows.

The dream turns this way, petal by petal, to face the halogen floodlights
that stream from the top of the water tower next to the cemetery.

We try to forget how small the hole was they dug for my uncle, now 28
pounds of ash

in a metal box, and this light that fills our faces blinds us, fills
our pockets, and every coin is a dark hero raising our dead into a kind

of afterlight, and the purpled green of grass stems in the cast shadows.
And the blue door again. Always the door and the dim entrance and the
soot and yellow bricks,

and inside a girl with a bun in her hair held by a paintbrush
and the ceiling split by the single bright line of florescent light.

The girl weaves sweetgrass into braids, bundles dried sage, drops
    her work on a blanket when the dancing begins.

And inside the dream I open my eyes and I'm no longer at Kyi-Yo
but at the Pow-Wow of Love in East Lansing, under the cold blue sky,

under the green steel rafters, and I'm dancing alone where all the
    Spartans wrestle
and I'm channeling that fury into pounding feet

and the Indians are cheering and stomping on the bleachers
and it's not the Hoop dance or the Fancydance

but the Hustle, a disco ball painting shooting stars across the floor,
and my hair, black like theirs now, and so long it wraps itself all the
    way around
the gymnasium.

Hawk in the Back Yard

Light feeds the plants that give us their seeds.
Farmers feed the fields

that give us their corn. Corn feeds the chickens
my mother eats.

My mother gives all the seeds
to the birds.

She can't spray the tree, or eat any apples,
because of a nest

high up in the branches, so
the apples feed the worms that live in the apples

and the wormy apples feed the deer
my stepdad tries to lure and then shoot,

but he doesn't try hard.
And lately

a hawk has been coming around
to eat all those birds.

But she doesn't stop feeding the birds
the hawk eats. Instead,

she buys more seeds.
Those birds need to be strong, she says,

and to grow up strong they need to eat
and she laughs,

and the birds and the corn
and the farmers and the seeds and my

stepdad all stop and listen, their eyes
on the high branch and the birdhouse

and the feeder and the sliding glass door
that leads to the kitchen.

The Self

What started as a dance
ends as a drink
the bar as long
as the tornadoed flagpole
 stretched across a city block
on your regular route.

Because the walls feel sorry
for you, they earth your
vibe with Jose Gonzales,
but you are none,
a speckled egg in the vat
too pickled to bloom.

But then, two famous poets
march like ants across the
stained linoleum with a message
for you in their pincers.
*Erase one tract of land
and put up another, like they*

*do in Brazil and Belize and
 like they did in Hawaii*, but
the irony escapes you, and
when your drink empties itself
the bartender escapes you, and the
ants escape you, yipping *yee-hoo*

through your spillage.
What else escapes?
Breath, from lips and noses.
Wood, from its prison
in the ground to its coffin in the
walls. Sound, as soon as it's done

being sound. But
not you. Over fries and ketchup
at The Ox you replenish the Self
into tomorrow, and ants move
from chamber to chamber, some of them
drunk now

because of you, the wood
cut from trees, burgers
from cows, drinks squeezed
from plants, and even right now, you
composed entirely, completely
of you.

The Blue Glow of

The warm electric hum of tubes
heating inside the box
is gone, flattened by scientists, and

the blue glow of
last years hydrangeas, gone,

hijacked to purple by some
dissident acid.

The bombed out church in Berlin,
the shape still stands,
a reminder, but

the anguish I used to feel
is gone, obliterated by the wrecking ball of

new wife, new child; therefore
the drinking buddies gone, the cigarettes,

well, one burns still
under the moons watchful eye,
real and hot in my lungs.

I throw it into the street,
into the past, I tell myself,

sneaking back in
quickly and quietly when I'm done.

Mars Rover Spirit, to Mars Rover Opportunity

I.

If only I could find you
in a different language.

In Spanish, all that separates
a horse from a gentleman
is a few letters.

Caballo. Caballero.

If only we could be this close,
in any small way.

I'll go on tricking myself
until I turn the same

dull and shocking red
as all this dust
and horizon.

II.

The mechanical groan
of my lens
rotating in its perpetual circle.

Every flutter in the air
when my eyes clack open
and shut.

The streaming video maker
gives a distorted moan
like a song underwater.

Every noise this endless field
can possibly carry to you.

The click and the two small beeps
after I send the maps
of my longing

on their own lonely journey
back to our creator, to that world.

III.

You must know that this place
is everything for us. The
polished flare of light

glinting off the
side panels wraps around
us like an atmosphere.

I can see you, rolling through it
on your toy wheels
on the other side

of this world, and I will never mistake you
for the scraps of some other
project.

But I can only hope
that one little glint of light
will find you,

that you can breath it,
feel it slip against your
tin panels,

that you know
what it means,
your horse here, your gentleman,
and praise the red dust,
and praise the red heaven.

The Much Love Sad Dawg Trio

I.

I don't know why I gave them this name
Translated from a language I can never decipher.

It seems an almost empty auditorium
Would feel less lonely

Than a completely empty one — but no —
And if you need to ask —

What would ___ do? —
You should try it with Ponce de Leon,
But beware the difference
Between Ponce before and Ponce after
He found eternal youth.

Beware your gutters don't sprout flowers
Like a delicate crown worn by your house.

Once, an African Violet friend of mine pushed out
One too many velvety purple blooms

And perished at the thought of being picked clean
Or sold at the farmer's market next to the mushroom guy,

The apple guy, the sweet cherry dangling
Like a dangerous proposition —

Two violins now, in perfect symmetry,
Beware the sadness underneath,

The cello,
The infinite configurations of a resolution.

II.

Days when I whisk through the halls
My head a fast cloud pushed by some invisible force

When the rooms drip with the alcohol swab scent
Of open markers,

I can become too large for any single word, any name –
Meanwhile the trio begins, and one poor sucker

Sits useless on the bench, the page turner,

He walks with his head low
As if he knows his hoi polloi place, but when the crowd breaks

Into applause at the end I bet his heart
Electrifies to neon, inviting us all

To that bright restaurant inside himself
Where the applause is all for him.

III.

I lied.
I do know why they gave me that name.

It's my name, given to me
By students who think I have everything to give to them –

I've been giving that name to other things
To see if it fits, to see

If I can see myself reflected
Everywhere, like a disco ball.

IV.

Sometimes I think it'd be easier to have
Inspector Gadget arms, arms on command, arms

By design, everywhere attainable opportunity.
Beware having too many

To choose—
What would Ponce do?

(What would Ponce do?)

V.

Much love sad dawg
Under the
Crazy moon
Howling

Like a dog
Out of luck, made
Vicious with
Endless

Sorry questions
About the
Dark center, the

Down low, below, while
Above us
Winking
Gods.

VI.

I am trying to make this fewer,
Lesser,

Without paint
Or shovel

Or nose
Or whale musk,

But everything drips a sobbing thrum, as if
They'd added

Another string
To the violin,

Another wheel
To the hot dog cart, another leg

To the dog across the street
In place of its tail, another mouth to eat

Another bowl to fill.

Everything spreads like peanut butter
To the edges of the bread,

By a knife by everyone's hand,
Leveling out in a human geology—

Once we stood tall, now we lie flat
In our slot, then we dissipate, dissolve

Into elements that build
The future into being.

VII.

I am lonely.
So I look around at other people and it helps.

When it doesn't, I browse
The electronics aisle

At the all night drug store
To see if anybody's invented the machine

That turns my name to neon
And invites the world inside again.

VIII.

Beware the moon, the stars, anything
That can be described as *vast*.

Beware the past, the paint, the words,
The attempts to find something vast.

Beware the light switch, the candle, the lamp.
Beware the poison you spread,

It's killing the ants.
Beware the ending. The piano's last note

Isn't it. You hum the song in your car
On the way home, memorize, remember, and smile.
Swear you'll never forget.

Vision

Nobody knows the limit
of a blue geranium, a blue
vista yawning its horizon,
the blue blue depths of an atom.

My neighbor with the landscaped
beard taught his son
to throw a baseball

all summer, and I had a vision
of him, the son, grown into a man,
throwing the ball some interminable,
galactic distance,

clearing, easily, the stratosphere
or whatever. Nobody knows the limit
of a vision.

Each day brings
paper flutes, a knot of wires, the long
smooth lines of a vent.
Each day the same bent man

hobbles over the cobblestone porch
toward his past, places
next to that monument

a cut flower and, next to that,
a live one.

Turning Thirty

I am capable of days like this
this gripping wind the optimists call
a *breeze*, the first snow
lighting up the block, and let's just say
the optimists are right for once, and leaving behind
me in my twenties and their biting sarcasm,
I look ahead to thirty, tomorrow,

and worry about my parents' mortality
and ignore my daughter's, start up a trust
and fill it with pennies and nickels each night, and
the never more than occasional dollar bill
wadded to pulp, and

let's just say the optimists are right
about everything; today, it's Optimist Day,
and waiting behind door number 2 is a mystery
so fantastic that hope cannot explain
its magnificence, only action, choice,

experience. The geologist tells us
the expanding Atlantic, the shrinking
Pacific. The philosopher tells us, in an
almost incomprehensible vernacular,
that all things matter in this one
peculiar way. In the meantime,

my infant daughter begins
to turn her head from side to side
and does it non-stop for three hours, as if
she were watching a tennis match,
back and forth, back and forth,
and I allow that cannibal

to taste me one more time before midnight,
and it's not hope or spirit or truth,
it's my daughter, learning, too early maybe,
that her version of things depends
on which way she looks.

In Accordance with the Prophecy

In accordance with the prophecy,
the teeth emerge at seven to nine months

in a flood of saliva so severe

the ark I've constructed
from bits of garage wood lashed together

by grape vine cut trying to choke
the chain link fence,

up to its neck now in water, fails us,

the ice caps gone now from the body heat
generated sleeping off

the double baby Tylenol dose
on my chest, the drool

streaming down our bodies until
it's half filled the room,

cupped the brim of the couch we lie on,

all hope of nicer, prettier hurricanes
like Dolly or Jane gone,

and don't even think about that vacation
to see the glaciers

before they leave us forever.

They've left.
The only thing to do now

is dream, build that imagination tower
thunk up by Sears and Disney and Yeats, that

escape hatch going up and
take me to a dry, barren place, the badlands

in one of the Dakotas
I drove through on my way to college,

or the Tucson desert, its gaunt
looming Saguaros standing guard

against flood, all that dry spiny life
ready to absorb its share. Once,

while hiking there, I came to a fence
in the middle of nowhere, separating

nothing from nothing.

And it's hard
to look down at that fence,

the green shoots from the dirt
barely peeking through,

to pray for each to live,

to eat the ones that grow.

Concert Posters

We walk the same block twice
each day, she struts

in her new pink pirate shirt,
then kneels like an army ranger

to point to the flag and the hoop
and the light-with-fire.

We keep adding new twists:
the yellow house with

the porch lamp, the big hill and hurdle,
taunting little Coco, whose mean

guttural snarls suggest
a thing more ferocious than she.

Near the end of the loop, past
the dumpster

in the parking lot cut-through,
we look in a music store's

tinted windows,
our half-reflections imposed

on concert posters, as if
they're advertising us to us,

coming soon to this block
this afternoon,

tickets cost
a thousand birds, a big truck,

this marigold bloom crushed
in our fists.

Faint Music

Maybe you need to see music
with your eyes, waves of notes

bending in the wind like wheat,

some crazy doppler of palm leaves
curving their sad cello.

A plywood box full of holes is an instrument

for the box stomper. So what else?
The news, that laser eye

on misery, its staccato ticker

a high-hat of destruction. The wine

green bottle of Jazz
for intellectuals who need an excuse.

Your neighbor's bicycle, white, too short

for its rider, hanging regardless
in the barn from a ceiling hook. A music

of not being used for its purpose.

Just look around and that's everywhere.

Which is not to say
it's not beautiful.

Because in the Movie They Got It All Wrong

You can't start with the line *I want to be in love* anymore. But
what if, inside the line, I listen for your footsteps in the
hall. Today you are staccato rumba, your coconut vistas

and treeless beaches glow. You use napkins to balance the
table. A friend of mine (several actually) uses pills. He
sees the world as a place *he* needs to adjust to, and

himself as the unprovoked knot in the wire. I say scratch the
tabletop into a kind of history. I say Mike wuz here. In
1968.

You can't start with the line *you are my lady* anymore. So why
bother? Maybe if everything worth doing has been done,
it's okay to repeat. And what if you did?

What if you *are* my lady? And our hands inside our hands
become a strange sort of language? I say give them their
language. Tattoo the cartoon heart on the top of your

chest. Say out loud what name will be in the banner. It still
won't be exactly what's underneath. In this way, a word
is only form, never actual. But, you say, what about the

word *word*? You say this in the silence between the little
clicks of your heels.

You say, you can't start with a woman dancing behind a wall.
Even if it's *this* wall. Better to start with a slow pan that
follows a long crack along the brick seams and ends

with a spray painted exclamation point. As long as it's purple,
you say. As long as you sign it with a sideways comma,
with two little dots above it for eyes.

Muting

Scribble several me's
onto a television

and call it episodes
of me.
There are so many explanations

for this. One,
there is more than one world

to love. Two, each word
depends on your choice.

Darwin
might hula through
the eye of a storm.

Elvis might practice worlding
in a mirror.

If they compete, one loses.
If not, nobody wins.
Therefore,

high school coaches are
everywhere,
cheerleaders no matter what.

Benediction

Thank you for the blue mosquito and the oily haze
and the new question that rises to my throat
as deep and piercing as a whale song.

And thank you for that night and the moon
in the window and the small falling scar of a palm tree
and the strung lights. And thank you for leaving me.

And thank you for the night you woke up and you
had a dream and you wouldn't tell me the dream.

I tried to give you something then. And thank you
for the skin and the register and the cup full of red pens.
And thank you for the friend that told me a dream

is only a lack. Or was that a ghost is a lack? Or was it all
that night in my mind like a scene from the movies. How

pale the skin from your body, and how glassy and cold. And
years later, how the cold seems less cold and less dangerous

and more true. And the one and only favor I can ask of you
is to pity me. And to thank me, too, for that night
and the light in this room and your image roiling away

like a small fog and my crawling skin. And how I feel lighter.
And how the weight of your body is gone. And how small
and delicate the memory is. And how blue and palpable.

When I come up with a new idea

When I come up with a new idea about the world
nobody hangs me from a pole
or banishes me from church and country
or mocks me in the Saturday night skit show.

I don't die penniless, alone, unappreciated
by my era or epoch or age and, wrong or not,
this makes me a little bit sad, even though

I see a man walking the sidewalk past Astoria
stopping to smell to rich butter cream air while
considering a move out here to the burbs.

He's hard at work on is latest invention —
not a machine but perpetual motion itself! —
when the idea hits him like a train and a lava lamp and a
Venn diagram and suddenly all of creation seems

possible and probable and certain and in his joy-gasm
he passes a beautiful woman and smiles at her
and she thinks he's just another ogling cretin checking out

her tits and fed up with this idiot America she cries out
Take a picture, Scumbag!
and immediately regrets not shouting something better
than that.

And the idea hits her, too, with the light and airy smell
of vanilla beans outside Astoria, the absolute, the *Arche*
of all comebacks, the perfect phrase to send him quivering

back into his slimy lair, but it's too late to turn and say it now
because the moment has already passed, the poor thing
dead before it was born.

When I come up with a new idea about the world
cows and chickens and pigs
are cut into strips, formed into patties, and offered locally
at a reasonable price to all my fellow humans; the earth warms to

no more winter and Florida beaches everywhere; I dream
and teach my unborn daughter how to dream
through the thin leather wall of Mary's belly.

I tell her the truth only, that the belly button
is a direct line to ask god questions, and that jelly beans were invented
just for her.

When I come up with a new idea about the world I put on my favorite tie
and unpack my chemistry set and combine
all the right molecules into all the proper formations

and mix it together with oil squeezed from the liver of endangered whales
to capture the essence of the idea and bottle it
and call it Sky and Passion and Beach Music and become
a fragrance millionaire!

When I come up with a new idea about the world
I will take a name befitting of one who comes up with such ideas about
    the world.
Heraclitus the Obscure rolled so correct.
So, too, will Sadler the Truthspreader, the Lover of Cookies.

And when I come up with a new idea about the world I sing you
to future sleep
these soft gray hours when the morning threatens to slow us.

A friend of mine came up with a new idea
about the world: a dream is only a lack, an absence,
some vital organ missing.

In one dream we fly over a long great wall I will teach you
how to dream about. Here's an idea:
What if everything I can give you, you already have, stitched
in your skin? What if you are too small to talk to, so I begin

by wagging some morse code at you with this one puppet finger,
an uncertain and infinite forever hello? I'll do anything;
I have to share this idea with you.

New Year's Pig

My joy is a sidewalk on the last small town parade
with the burning reds of changing maples

and the brassy doppler of a far off band

and the Shriners in their Devo hats and zippy
little cars. If my world is tilted, this street

is its axis. I didn't come here for answers,

only to hear a chorus of sealed lips
humming *Louie Louie!* and *The Final Countdown*
and *The Heat Is On*. I didn't come here

to *feel* joy so much as to give myself

away. Sitting in my sagging Adirondack
under the blooming hub of a wire pole, I see

a solitary ant carrying the nacho-orange tip
of a Dorito to its own celebration.

If I close my eyes now I know I'll miss out
on the next Miss Golden Rose but

there are so many other things I can see.

First, I'm in Coleraine next to the giant grasses
on the road to Portsrush. Or I'm inside

the dark and seedy VFW on Pine, stuffing

hard boiled eggs one after another into
my parched gullet. Or I'm in Detroit again,

on a different street, another axis, walking a route
I'd mastered through a summer of boredom.

After I imagine death as a symphony of leaves
scraping the road, I pass four hulking steam vents
topped by massive steel grey nipples and

beyond them I see two kids, you know
they are beautiful, throwing a ball through a milk crate,

the same ancient game forever. They taunt me

from their stoop, the sunlight smashes me
off their smiling teeth. One great man said

love your fate and ended in tears, apologizing
to a horse. Can you see his ghost hovering
above the towns and fields and city streets?

Does he see me here, smiling back at the perfect
faces, forgiving my trespassers,

the unmistakable murmur of leaves
in the stiff wind, the sharp angles of architecture

breaking the soft curve of the horizon.

Those leaves are the people humming
around me, and if I open my eyes now I'll see

dancing, even the most threadbare of toughs

bobbing their heads at least, even the pig
marching down the avenue toward its final
canvas tent, leashed by a heavy rope

to its captors, sticking its snout into the air
like us, curious, building itself into a moment,

loving every moment of the moment
and somehow stalling the future, slowing down

time, overcoming its fate.

About the Author

Matt Sadler lives with his wife and kids in the suburbs of Detroit, where he teaches writing and film.

DYNAMO VERLAG BOOKS

Telescopes and Other People
JOSH NORMAN

Peregrine Nation
LUCIAN MATTISON

The Much Love Sad Dawg Trio
MATT SADLER

Chansons Russes
CALEB TRUE

DYNAMOVERLAG.COM

www.ingramcontent.com/pod-product-compliance
Lightning Source LLC
Chambersburg PA
CBHW060538080526
44586CB00012B/787